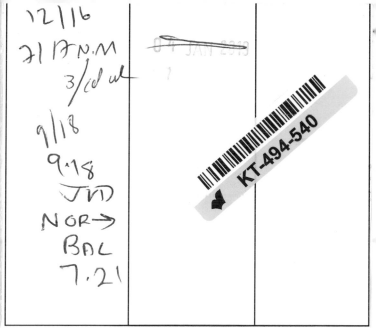

THE LITTLE BOOK OF VEGANISM

Summersdale Publishers Ltd
46 West Street
Chichester
West Sussex
PO1    1RP
UK

www

Print

ISBN   9030 00005 3258 5

Subst
corpo
Nicky
email

# Contents

# Introduction

Welcome to *The Little Book of Veganism*. Maybe you've picked this up because you're curious about the vegan lifestyle; maybe you have friends and family who are vegan and you'd like to know more. Whatever your reason, this little book is designed to give you bite-size pieces of information to help you learn what veganism is, why people live the lifestyle and how it can work for you. There are also lots of recipes and recommendations to ensure that your move to veganism is a smooth one.

# INTELLIGENCE IS THE ABILITY OF A SPECIES TO LIVE IN HARMONY WITH ITS ENVIRONMENT.

## PAUL WATSON

# WHAT VEGANISM MEANS: A BRIEF Q&A

HERE ARE SOME COMMON
QUESTIONS ABOUT VEGANISM
THAT YOU, OR PEOPLE YOU
WILL TALK TO, MAY HAVE.

# WHY NOT MILK?

Many people say that they understand the choice to be vegetarian, but that they don't see the problem with milk.

Whilst it is true that milk does not directly kill the animal it is taken from, the dairy industry is, unfortunately, cruel. Cows are kept in confined conditions, even on organic farms, and repeatedly artificially inseminated to keep them producing milk. Their calves are taken from them seconds after birth – females to have the same fate as their mothers, and males usually to become veal.

Aside from the issue of cruelty, milk simply isn't designed for the human body. Cows' milk is designed to make a calf grow large quickly, not to add to the health of a human being. Approximately 75 per cent of the world's population is intolerant to lactose, and the calcium contained in milk can be hard for the human body to access because of the acidifying nature of milk. In short, milk is not a necessary addition to a balanced diet.

There are many great alternatives on the market; it doesn't just stop at soya milk – almond, hazelnut and coconut milks are particularly flavoursome and popular, and many are enriched with calcium and vitamins. These days, even cheese is fairly easy to replace, with improved vegan-friendly and non-dairy cheeses coming on to the market all the time.

# All About Veganism

Donald Watson, founder of The Vegan Society, coined the term 'vegan' in 1944. He said the word represented 'the beginning and end of vegetarian'.

# BUT WHAT ABOUT EGGS?

In many cultures, it is not considered vegetarian to eat eggs. In the West, eggs are sold to us as a high-protein food, with a complete amino-acid profile, which is inherently good for us. However, this is not true.

Though there is much debate about how many eggs one should eat in a week, it is worth considering whether they are a good food source at all. Like milk, eggs are designed to be a food source for the chicks that would grow inside them, not for human beings.

Added to this, the egg industry is cruel. Even 'free range' eggs generally come from hens who hardly see the light of day, live in cramped conditions, and have been bred to produce eggs at far beyond their natural rate, meaning their bodies wear out quickly, giving them short, unhappy lives. Eggs are not a necessary food, and are not even needed for baking. It is simple to replace eggs in a cake and still have a moist and delicious treat. Mashed banana, for example, is a wonderful – and healthy – egg replacement, as is apple sauce. Flaxseed can be used as a binder too, and adds extra protein.

# HONEY, I NEED SOMETHING SWEET

Honey is a subject of much debate, with some people who call themselves vegan still consuming it, along with other bee products such as honeycomb or bee pollen.

The reason honey is not considered vegan is primarily that it is an animal by-product, and that bees are exploited and often damaged by its production. Even small-sized producers and hobbyists often subject their bees to cruelty, such as cutting off the queen's wings so that she can't swarm.

If you want a sweet alternative to drizzle on your soya yoghurt, or to add to tea, try agave nectar, which comes from a cactus. Date syrup or rice syrup are also good alternatives.

# ONE SHOULD NOT KILL A LIVING BEING, NOR CAUSE IT TO BE KILLED, NOR SHOULD ONE INCITE ANOTHER TO KILL. DO NOT INJURE ANY BEING, EITHER STRONG OR WEAK, IN THE WORLD.

BUDDHA

# BUT DON'T I NEED DAIRY PRODUCTS FOR CALCIUM?

We have touched on the issues surrounding dairy products already, but many people will be worried about getting enough calcium. This mineral is needed for healthy bones and teeth, and many of us have been told from childhood that milk is the best place to find calcium. Well, along with around 75 per cent of the world's population being unable to digest lactose, making milk far from an ideal foodstuff, there are plenty of places to get your calcium from in a plant-based diet.

Calcium is present in many plant foods, particularly leafy green vegetables, such as kale. These veggies have the added benefit of containing a plethora of other, complementary vitamins and minerals for optimum health. Almonds are also a good source of calcium, along with sesame seeds, tofu and soya milk. Indeed, many plant-based milks and yoghurts are also fortified, so calcium isn't something you need to worry about when eating a balanced vegan diet.

# PROTEIN, THOUGH

One of the top questions vegans are asked is: 'But where do you get your protein?!'

The idea that 'protein' is a specific food group is incorrect. Protein is found in smaller or larger proportions in many different foods; even potatoes contain protein.

The main thing to remember is that you need to consume all nine of the essential amino acids to ensure you get everything you need to maintain a healthy body. All nine can be found in plant-based foods, so a balanced vegan diet provides you with everything you need. Indeed, some plant foods have a complete amino-acid profile, such as quinoa, buckwheat, chia and hemp, as well as fermented soya bean products. Other particularly rich sources of protein for a vegan diet include beans, lentils and nuts, as well as tofu and seitan ('wheat meat'). One of the simplest ways to have a protein-rich meal, with a complete amino-acid profile, is to eat rice and beans. Delicious.

# YOU CAN JUDGE A MAN'S TRUE CHARACTER BY THE WAY HE TREATS HIS FELLOW ANIMALS.

PAUL McCARTNEY

# GET YOUR VITAMINS

Some may worry that they will miss out on essential vitamins and minerals if they are not consuming meat, fish, eggs or dairy products. This is, however, not the case. A balanced vegan diet will generally give a higher vitamin boost than a standard meat-based or vegetarian diet, because the focus is on plants. And you don't need a steak for your iron – kale is far richer in the essential mineral, and easier on the stomach.

One thing to look out for is vitamin $B_{12}$. This appears in meat and dairy due to supplements being fed to animals, and people then eating the supplemented animals or their by-products. Grass-fed animals get their $B_{12}$ naturally, as they eat soil when they consume greenery, and the bacteria in soil produce $B_{12}$. Eating veg that hasn't been scrubbed can help boost your $B_{12}$. Vegans should make sure they consume fortified foods so they do not miss out on this essential vitamin. Or, if your diet won't contain enough fortified foods, take a supplement (there are plenty of vegan-safe options on the market).

# WOOL IS FINE, RIGHT?

Many think that being vegan is just about diet, but living a truly cruelty-free lifestyle means saying no to wool and leather. As it is made from the skin of dead animals, the reasons for not wearing leather are obvious. Wool is a little more complex. Sadly for sheep, the wool taken from them is not just a little haircut – they are sheared as close to the skin as possible, so the maximum amount of fleece is taken. This means that for many sheep, cuts, grazes and even loss of skin are common.

Add to this the fact that the sheep who are not producing enough wool are funnelled into the meat industry, often exported alive, and you'll see that wool use inherently supports the killing of animals.

There are many other natural fibres that can prove just as soft and warm – even cotton – so why not try switching? (It may also prove less itchy!)

# SMOOTH AS SILK

Silk is often seen as a luxury commodity, and its soft, lightweight nature makes it a very popular option, particularly for women's clothing. However, silk is not produced by happy silkworms. Indeed, cocooned silkworms are boiled alive so that their silken creations can be unravelled and used to create fabric.

Consider viscose as an alternative option for silky-soft clothes. This can even be made from pine fibre, so it is cruelty-free and often still natural.

# *All About Veganism*

The first known vegan cookbook, written by Rupert H. Wheldon and titled *No Animal Food: Two Essays and 100 Recipes*, was published in 1910.

# BUT I HEARD THAT PLANTS FEEL PAIN, TOO?

While some recent research has suggested that plants may have a form of nervous system and 'feel pain' when plucked from the soil, this is no reason to continue using meat and animal products. Though plants *may* feel some degree of pain – and this has in no way been proven – it is known that animals do feel pain and emotion. Think of it this way: would you compare picking some daisies to killing a garden bird? It is likely that your answer is no, and the same goes for farmed animals.

If you are convinced plants feel pain, consider the fact that by eating meat you are killing more plants, as well as the animal itself. Farmed animals are fed a huge amount of plant matter before being slaughtered – certainly more than a vegan could eat on their own – so in eating meat you are essentially doubling your plant destruction. Further, this extra use of plants for meat production means that more land is given over to the arable farming of certain crops, thus destroying wild animals' habitat.

# All About Veganism

It takes over 4,000 gallons of water to produce a day's worth of food for a meat eater; it takes only 1,200 gallons of water for a lacto-ovo-vegetarian and only 300 gallons for a vegan.

# BUT ISN'T EATING MEAT WHAT MADE US EVOLVE?

There have been studies which suggest that cooking and eating meat is what made us evolve to be the highly intelligent creatures we are today. Other studies, though, have suggested it was the eating of high-energy grain foods. As these involve looking back hundreds of thousands of years, they are essentially conjecture.

If it is the case that the cooking and eating of meat gave us a boost, there is every possibility we turned to it because other food sources were lacking. A temporary need – not a necessity. Further, we modern humans do not have this need as we can get everything we require from plant foods, and have the capacity for compassion that should allow us to view other animals with respect.

Another aspect of this argument is that, since our ancestors ate this way, so should we (a viewpoint put forward by followers of the Palaeo diet). However, using this argument, many other atrocities could be considered reasonable, such as selling women into marriage, burning witches at the stake, bear-baiting or even slavery. Just because something has been done in the past, that does not mean we have to continue doing it in the future.

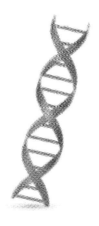

# OUR TEETH ARE DESIGNED FOR MEAT-EATING THOUGH, AREN'T THEY?

The short answer to this question is: no. Our sharper teeth often get referred to as 'canines', but really they bear very little resemblance to actual canine (or feline) teeth. Our teeth are mostly blunt, for grinding plants and grains, and the sharper ones more likely developed for ripping the skins of tougher fruits, as in many other apes. Some of these apes do occasionally eat meat, and their teeth can help with this, but for many this behaviour is opportunistic and not a part of their usual diet. In short, our teeth give us the ability to rip meat apart, but they do not show we were 'designed' to eat it.

# WHAT ABOUT LIONS?

A surprisingly large number of people seem to think that because lions (or wolves, or some other wild animals) eat meat, that means we should, too. It's true that not every animal on this planet can be vegan. Cats, for example, are obligate carnivores, meaning that they need nutrition from meat to thrive. Humans are not.

As well as the fact that meat is necessary for lions, and unnecessary for humans, it should be noted that citing a wild animal as a point of reference is flawed. Lions also kill other males' young when they mate, so should humans do that, too? If your answer is 'of course not', then try to apply the same logic to meat-eating.

# ANIMALS... WERE NOT MADE FOR HUMANS ANY MORE THAN BLACK PEOPLE WERE MADE FOR WHITE, OR WOMEN CREATED FOR MEN.

## ALICE WALKER

# CAN ONE PERSON REALLY MAKE A DIFFERENCE?

You truly can! Going vegan is just a set of small changes that will most likely have only positive effects on you, and which will have a profoundly positive effect on the world around you. Just one example: as a vegan, you use far less water (this could be a 50 per cent reduction) than someone who eats meat and dairy. Further, if you think one person going vegan doesn't make much difference to animals, think about this: during one year alone, on average, a vegan will save the lives of 198 animals through not eating meat. Over ten years, that's 1,980 animals who won't lose their lives. That's no mean feat.

# BUT WHAT ABOUT THE THIRD WORLD?

Some people feel that going vegan is all well and good if you are wealthy and can buy 'specialist' foods, but believe that for poorer people it is too difficult. For this reason, they feel there is 'no point' going vegan.

The opposite to this is, in fact, true. Though there are many specialist foods available to those in the developed world, a healthy vegan diet requires only natural, plant-based foods, which are abundant and cheap. Rice and beans are certainly not expensive and in many poorer countries provide the staple diet. In India, for example, vegetarians and vegans make up around 40 per cent of the population.

# WHAT DO YOU EVEN EAT?!

Quite simply, anything that isn't an animal and doesn't come from one! There are many varieties of fruit, vegetables, beans, nuts, rice and pasta, and other foodstuffs that can make up a healthy vegan diet. If you find the transition tricky, there are also many meat alternatives or 'mock meats' on the market, which can help you eat meals you're used to, with just a small change. Indeed, many people find that going vegan makes them more likely to experiment with their cooking as they try new things. Why not try out some of the recipes in this book, to see just how easy eating a vegan diet can be?

# WE CANNOT HAVE PEACE AMONG MEN WHOSE HEARTS FIND DELIGHT IN KILLING ANY LIVING CREATURE.

RACHEL CARSON

# BREAKFAST
# AND BRUNCH

WHEN FRIED EGGS OR A
BACON SANDWICH ARE NO
LONGER AN OPTION, WHAT DO
YOU EAT FOR BREAKFAST?
AND SURELY PANCAKES ARE
OUT OF THE QUESTION?
WELL, HERE ARE SOME DELICIOUS
RECIPES FOR BREAKFAST TREATS
THAT ANYONE CAN ENJOY.

# FABULOUS FRUIT SALAD

FRUIT DOESN'T JUST HAVE TO BE
A SNACK, AND IT DOESN'T HAVE TO BE
DULL, EITHER. TRY PUTTING THIS TOGETHER
AND DRIZZLING IT WITH AGAVE NECTAR, OR
EATING IT WITH SOME SOYA YOGHURT AND A
SPRINKLING OF YOUR FAVOURITE GRANOLA.

## INGREDIENTS

**1 banana, chopped**

**A handful of fresh strawberries, quartered**

**A handful of fresh raspberries**

**A handful of fresh blueberries**

Simply mix the banana and berries together for a vitamin-rich and delicious breakfast treat.

If you fancy something different, try adding pineapple or melon into the mix, or even adding a sprinkling of crunchy mixed seeds.

# PERFECT PANCAKES

THESE ARE THE CRÊPE-STYLE PANCAKES YOU
MIGHT EAT ON SHROVE TUESDAY. NO NEED FOR
THE EGGS. IF YOU ARE NOT A FAN OF SOYA,
COCONUT MILK OR UNSWEETENED ALMOND
MILK CAN ALSO BE USED IN THIS RECIPE.

# INGREDIENTS

**1 cup plain flour**

**¼ cup soft brown sugar**

**1½ teaspoons arrowroot (available in the supermarket baking aisle with the baking powder and cornflour)**

**1 cup plain soya milk**

**Coconut oil (for frying)**

Place the flour, sugar and arrowroot in a mixing bowl and mix together with a fork or whisk. Add the milk, half a cup at a time, stirring constantly to form a smooth batter. If the mixture looks a little thick, add a drop more soya milk.

Once your batter is ready, heat a little coconut oil in a non-stick pan. Use a ladle or a ⅓ cup to spoon batter into the pan. For each pancake, swirl the batter, or use a spatula to spread it, so that it covers the base of the pan.

Turn the pancake once the edges start to curl up, or when there is no more raw batter visible – after about 1 minute. Cook for around another 30 seconds on the other side, then slide out of the pan on to a plate.

Repeat this for each pancake. This batter mixture makes around six pancakes.

To serve, why not try some of your favourites like chocolate spread and banana (Plamil make an excellent non-dairy chocolate spread), or sugar and lemon.

I JUST COULDN'T STAND
THE IDEA OF EATING MEAT
— I REALLY DO THINK THAT
[STOPPING] IT HAS MADE
ME CALMER.

KATE BUSH

# BACON SANDWICH? YES, YOU CAN

Not so much a recipe but a suggestion. There are various veggie-bacon varieties around, and though none of them tastes quite like the bacon you might remember, they have a savoury, smoky flavour that works well in a sandwich with some ketchup or brown sauce. Tempeh 'bacon', made of seasoned and fermented soya beans, is one of the healthiest, with a strong amino-acid profile. It can also be sliced to add to various other recipes.

Coconut can even be made into a tasty bacon substitute; there are lots of recipes online just waiting to be tried.

# SUPER GREEN SMOOTHIE

ANOTHER GREAT, SIMPLE GO-TO FOR BREAKFAST, PACKED WITH FLAVOUR AND NUTRIENTS. SIMPLY TAKE YOUR CHOICE OF GREENS AND FRUITS, TOP WITH WATER AND BLEND. AROUND A QUARTER SHOULD BE MADE UP OF GREENS. I WOULD RECOMMEND A HIGH-POWERED BLENDER FOR THESE, AS WE WANT TO USE THE WHOLE FRUIT OR VEGETABLE. YOU CAN EVEN MAKE SMOOTHIES EXTRA CREAMY BY ADDING NUTS, SUCH AS CASHEWS, INTO THE MIX. THESE CAN ALSO BE A GREAT SNACK — WHY NOT TRY ONE OF THE COMBINATIONS SUGGESTED, OR USE YOUR OWN FAVOURITES?

## INGREDIENTS

### Classic

Spinach

Banana

Strawberries

### Melba

Spinach or romaine
lettuce

Banana

Nectarine or peach

Raspberries

### Tropical

Kale or spinach

Melon

Pineapple

Kiwi

Banana

### Berry nice

Spinach

Banana

Strawberries

Raspberries

Blueberries

# All About Veganism

Several studies have shown that vegans have lower rates of cancer, obesity, diabetes and hypertension, and that after just a couple of months a vegan diet can cause cancer-preventing genes to turn on, and cancer-causing genes to turn off.

# VEGGIE SCRAMBLE A-GO-GO

IF YOU MISS SCRAMBLED EGGS, OR OMELETTES, THIS IS A GREAT PLACE TO START. YOU CAN EITHER EAT THIS AS IT IS WITH A COOKED BREAKFAST, OR ON TOAST, OR YOU CAN COMBINE IT WITH VEGGIES, EITHER LOOSE, OR PRESSED INTO A PAN AND BAKED TO MAKE A TOFU OMELETTE.

## INGREDIENTS

**1 pack firm tofu (not silken), pressed**

**¼ cup nutritional yeast**

**1 teaspoon wholegrain mustard (or to taste)**

**1 teaspoon garlic puree (or to taste)**

**1 teaspoon turmeric powder**

**Pinch of salt and/or dash of soya sauce/Bragg's liquid aminos**

**Oil for frying (olive, or other neutral-tasting oil)**

**Veggies of choice (optional)**

First, chop the pressed tofu, then mash with a fork. Some lumps are fine – we are looking for scrambled-egg-esque consistency.

Next, add the other ingredients and mix well, continuing to mash together.

Once everything is mixed, heat a little oil in a non-stick pan and cook for around 10 minutes, until warm through.

Serve with your choice of veggies, on toast or with a cooked breakfast.

This can even be used as part of the filling for a breakfast burrito.

# AN ANIMAL'S EYES HAVE THE POWER TO SPEAK A GREAT LANGUAGE.

MARTIN BUBER

# WHAT'S FOR DINNER?

WHO NEEDS MEAT AND
TWO VEG?! HERE ARE
SOME DELICIOUS, SIMPLE
OPTIONS FOR YOU TO TRY.

# CHILLI NON CARNE

CHILLI IS A FIRM FAVOURITE IN MANY HOUSEHOLDS, AND THIS MIXED-BEAN VARIETY IS TASTY AND FILLING — WITH NOT A COW IN SIGHT!

# INGREDIENTS

Olive oil (for frying)

1 onion, finely chopped

3 cloves garlic, finely chopped

1 pepper (any colour will do), cubed

5 – 8 mushrooms, sliced

1–2 chillies, finely chopped

1 can black beans, drained and rinsed

1 can kidney beans, drained and rinsed

1 can baked beans

1 can chopped tomatoes

Chilli powder (to taste)

Black pepper (to taste)

Cayenne pepper (to taste)

Hot sauce (to taste)

Heat the olive oil in a large pan and add the chopped onion, cooking gently until it starts to soften. Add the garlic and cook for another minute. Add the peppers and mushrooms, cooking until just soft. Next, add the chillies, stirring through well. Then add the black beans and kidney beans, followed by the baked beans (the tomato sauce is a great cheat to add extra thickness and flavour). Stir in the chopped tomatoes, and season according to taste.

This can simmer for up to half an hour, but needs at least 15-20 minutes.

Serve with brown rice and sliced avocado for a complete, delicious meal.

If you'd like to try something different, seitan sausage, sliced finely and added with the mushrooms, is a great addition. (Seitan is 'wheat meat' and the sausages can be bought online and in many health food shops.)

# All About Veganism

Alternative names for those who followed an animal-free diet suggested by early members of The Vegan Society included allvega, neo-vegetarian, dairyban, vitan, benevore, sanivores and beaumangeur.

# ROASTED BEETROOT RISOTTO

THIS DISH ADDS A GORGEOUS SPLASH
OF COLOUR TO YOUR DINING, AND IS
WONDERFULLY FILLING. INGREDIENT
AMOUNTS CAN BE JUDGED ACCORDING
TO PERSONAL TASTE.

## INGREDIENTS

**2 large beetroots, peeled and chopped roughly into cubes**

**Olive oil**

**Balsamic vinegar**

**1 small red onion, finely chopped**

**Risotto rice**

**White wine**

**Vegetable stock**

**Nutritional yeast**

**Black pepper**

Place the beetroot cubes in an oven dish and drizzle with olive oil and a grind of black pepper. Roast for 20 minutes, or until it starts to soften, then drizzle with balsamic vinegar and roast for another 20 minutes, or until completely cooked through.

Heat more olive oil in a non-stick pan and fry the onion gently, softening but not colouring it. Add the risotto rice (using the packet instructions for quantities) and stir through, cooking it in the oil for a few minutes.

Next, add the white wine (enough to cover the rice) and allow to cook off, whilst stirring.

Continue to stir, then add your hot vegetable stock, ladle by ladle, adding more when the rice has absorbed the previous amount.

Close to the end of cooking, when the rice is beginning to become soft, add the beetroot along with its balsamic juices and continue to stir through. You may need to keep adding stock to make sure the rice is cooked through.

The risotto will be ready when the rice is slightly al dente and the sauce still loose. Stir a little nutritional yeast through at the end, for a cheesy flavour.

Great served with a crisp salad or crusty bread.

# TASTY TOFU STEAKS

PERFECT FOR IF YOU WANT A 'MEATY' MEAL.

# INGREDIENTS

**Firm tofu (not silken)**

**Your favourite barbecue/jerk sauce/marinade**

**Potatoes and veggies (to serve)**

This is an extremely easy meal, and just requires time and patience for the tofu.

Press the tofu for at least an hour, preferably overnight. To do this, either use a tofu press, or wrap the drained tofu in kitchen roll and place on a plate, placing another plate on top, with something heavy (such as a large can) on the top plate. If the kitchen roll becomes soaked through, remove it and re-wrap the tofu.

Once the tofu is ready, slice it in half to form two 'steaks'. With a larger piece, you could cut it into four. Place the steaks in a dish and smother with your preferred sauce or marinade, leaving for at least an hour.

Once ready, place on a baking tray and bake in the oven at 180°C for around 20 minutes, or until crispy and glazed on the outside.

Serve with your choice of potatoes and veggies, such as new potatoes drizzled with olive oil, and corn on the cob.

# THERE IS NO FUNDAMENTAL DIFFERENCE BETWEEN MAN AND ANIMALS IN THEIR ABILITY TO FEEL PLEASURE AND PAIN, HAPPINESS, AND MISERY.

## CHARLES DARWIN

# All About Veganism

The food consumed by the world's cattle is equal to the calorific needs of 8.7 billion people – over a billion more than the world's current human population.

# MINESTRONE-STYLE SOUP

A HEARTY SOUP WITH TOMATOES
AND PASTA — FILLING ON ITS OWN,
OR GREAT WITH BREAD.

## INGREDIENTS

Olive oil (for frying)

1 large onion, finely chopped

3 cloves garlic, minced

1 red pepper, diced

1 courgette, chopped into small pieces

5–8 mushrooms, sliced or quartered

1 can chopped tomatoes

1 litre vegetable stock

Black pepper (to taste)

1 can cannellini beans, drained and rinsed

Mixed herbs (to taste)

Chilli flakes (to taste)

1–2 handfuls small pasta, e.g. conchigliette

Heat the olive oil in a large, non-stick pan. Fry the onion until soft, then add the garlic. Add the pepper, courgette and mushrooms, and cook until just soft. Add the tin of tomatoes, the beans and the stock. Season to taste and let it simmer for 10 minutes.

Next, add the pasta. Continue to simmer, stirring regularly, until the pasta is soft.

Serve in big bowls with garlicky bread.

# SUPERB STIR-FRY

STIR-FRYING IS SUCH A SIMPLE WAY TO GET SO MUCH GOODNESS. THE VEGETABLES SUGGESTED CAN BE REPLACED WITH ANY OF YOUR FAVOURITES, FOR MORE BITE, YOU COULD ADD TOFU, TEMPEH OR MOCK MEATS.

# INGREDIENTS

Coconut oil (for frying)

Sesame oil

One onion, sliced

One carrot, sliced in batons

One courgette, sliced in batons

Mushrooms, chopped

A red, yellow or green pepper, sliced in batons

One red chilli, finely chopped

Two garlic cloves, finely chopped

Rice wine vinegar

Soy sauce

Start by heating the coconut oil in your wok (if you don't have a wok, a deep-frying pan can also be used). Once the coconut oil has melted, add the sesame oil.

Next, add the onion and fry until slightly soft. Then add each vegetable, one at a time, stirring as you go. Stir-fry until all veggies are cooked enough, then add the seasonings, using the rice wine vinegar and soy sauce to taste.

Serve over noodles or rice, and enjoy!

# I DECIDED TO PICK THE DIET THAT I THOUGHT WOULD MAXIMIZE MY CHANCES OF LONG-TERM SURVIVAL.

## AL GORE ON BECOMING VEGAN

# SWEET TREATS

'BUT I'LL MISS CAKE!' NO, YOU WON'T! YOU CAN HAVE YOUR VEGAN CAKE AND EAT IT. HERE IS A HANDFUL OF DELICIOUS DESSERTS YOU CAN WHIP UP IN NO TIME. ENJOY!

# BEST BROWNIES

THESE TOFU-BASED BROWNIES ARE
MOIST AND DELICIOUS. BAKED LONGER,
THEY ARE MORE CRUMBLY.

# INGREDIENTS

⅓ pack silken tofu (such as mori-nu)

¼ cup almond milk

½ cup rapeseed oil (or other neutral-tasting oil)

1 cup golden caster sugar

3 teaspoons vanilla extract

1 cup plain flour

½ cup cocoa

1 tablespoon cornflour

½ teaspoon baking powder

Pinch of salt

Dark or dairy-free chocolate chunks or chips
(optional)

Preheat your oven to 180°C and line a square brownie tin
with baking paper.

In a blender, blend the tofu, milk and oil together so that they form a sort of mayonnaise, then transfer to a large mixing bowl, making sure you get as much of the mix out as possible.

Mix in the sugar and vanilla, then add the dry ingredients and mix well. If using chocolate chunks, now is the time to stir them through.

Transfer the mix to your baking tin, and bake for around half an hour.

Let it cool for at least 15 minutes before slicing and enjoying.

# All About Veganism

Stricter variations of veganism include fruitarianism, which consists mostly of culinary fruits, seeds and nuts, and raw veganism, which is a vegan diet with all food eaten in its raw state.

# LOW-GLUTEN BANANA AND CHOCOLATE MUFFINS

WITH THEIR FRUIT AND LOWER
GLUTEN CONTENT, SURELY THESE
ARE ACTUALLY HEALTHY?

## INGREDIENTS

2 cups plain flour

2½ cups gluten-free flour blend (such as Doves Farm)

1 teaspoon bicarbonate of soda

1 teaspoon baking powder

1¼ cups golden caster sugar

2 ripe bananas, mashed

1½ cups almond milk (or soya milk)

1⅓ cups rapeseed oil (or other neutral-tasting oil)

2 teaspoons vanilla extract

½ bar dark or dairy-free chocolate, broken into chunks (or equivalent chocolate chips)

Preheat your oven to 180°C. Line your muffin tray with cases.

In a mixing bowl, mix the dry ingredients together. Add the bananas, milk, oil and vanilla and mix so everything has just come together. Then add your chocolate chunks and stir through so they are evenly distributed. Don't worry if there are a few lumps in your mix.

Spoon the mix into the waiting cases and bake for around 22 minutes.

Let the muffins cool for at least 10 minutes before enjoying them.

# All About Veganism

Producing just half a kilogram of meat requires up to 8 kilograms of grain.

# SIMPLE POACHED PEARS

FRUIT FOR DESSERT? THIS ELEVATES FRUIT
TO NEW HEIGHTS OF DELICIOUSNESS.

# INGREDIENTS

**Golden caster sugar**

**Vegan red wine**

**A cinnamon stick**

**Seeds from 1 vanilla pod (or teaspoon vanilla extract)**

**2 sprigs fresh thyme**

**4 pears, peeled but whole**

The amount of sugar and wine depends on: a) your taste and b) the size of your pan – you will need to cover the pears with liquid.

Put all ingredients except the pears into a non-stick pan and start to heat through. When the sugar has dissolved, add the pears and allow to simmer in the liquid for around 20 minutes. Remove the pears, then let the liquid boil down to form a syrup.

Serve the pears with a little of the syrup. They are also great accompanied by dairy-free ice cream or cream.

# N'ICE CREAM

This is possibly the simplest recipe for ice cream you will ever find. It doesn't even need an ingredients list.

Simply chop and freeze some ripe bananas. When you fancy ice cream, take them from the freezer, blend until smooth and serve.

To make other flavours, simply add other fruits or sauces when blending, for example dairy-free chocolate sauce, agave syrup and cinnamon, strawberries or vanilla essence. Simple and delicious, this dessert can be eaten as it is, or served as an accompaniment, such as with brownies.

# BECOMING VEGAN IS THE MOST IMPORTANT AND DIRECT CHANGE WE CAN IMMEDIATELY MAKE TO SAVE THE PLANET AND ITS SPECIES.

CHRIS HEDGES

# HINTS AND TIPS

WE'VE LOOKED A LOT AT FOOD BUT, AS YOU NOW KNOW, VEGANISM ISN'T JUST ABOUT WHAT YOU EAT. HERE, YOU'LL FIND HINTS AND TIPS ABOUT OTHER ASPECTS OF THE VEGAN LIFESTYLE, SUCH AS HOUSEHOLD CARE, COSMETICS AND SHOPPING.

# BUY NATURAL

When looking to convert your household products to veganism, one of the easiest things to do is opt for natural products. Companies producing natural household cleaning and care products tend to be more ethically and environmentally focused, so they use plant-based, non-toxic ingredients.

In natural products, the things to look out for that could make them non-vegan include honey and beeswax. Make sure you buy BUAV-approved products, so you know they have not been tested on animals.

# All About Veganism

A number of studies have shown that a vegan diet can increase a person's metabolism. In the first three hours after a meal, the body burns calories up to 16 per cent faster on a vegan diet than on a meat-based diet.

# MINERAL MAKE-UP

One of the simplest ways to make sure your make-up bag is all vegan is to opt for pure mineral make-up, which is often better for your skin and clogs the pores less. Not only will this be cruelty free and natural, but in most cases it will also be free from any animal-derived ingredients.

Be on the lookout for beeswax, carmines, silk and animal fats, all of which can make their way into make-up products. Carmine dyes are particularly common, especially in red and purple colours, and are made by boiling scale insects – not the most glamorous thing to put on your face!

# BUY ORGANIC

Buying organic fruit, veg and even clothing is not strictly part of a vegan lifestyle, but it is beneficial both for you and for animals in many ways.

Organic crops are grown without pesticides, so are kinder to the insects that roam the countryside. High-chemical agriculture kills off many insects, including extremely important bees. This has a knock-on effect for wildlife: with no insects to hunt, many birds and small mammals lose their food source and their homes.

It also means you won't be taking harsh chemicals into your body, that you will receive more vitamins and minerals, and that your fruit and veg won't require as much washing.

Box schemes which deliver high-quality organic products, available all over the country, make buying organic a far more affordable and viable option than ever before.

# SHOP SECOND-HAND AND VINTAGE

Another lifestyle choice that's not a vegan prerequisite by any means, but shopping second-hand and vintage helps preserve the environment by saving items from landfill, and means your money is going to small businesses, individuals or charities, rather than big corporations (which may test products on animals or have wasteful practices that harm the environment).

Second-hand shops are also helpful when making the transition to a vegan lifestyle. If you decide you'd like to get rid of any leather, silk, suede or cashmere products already in your wardrobe, why not give them to charity? It means the products won't go to waste (and may even stop someone else buying new animal-based products, thus decreasing the demand for them) and your conscience will be clear!

# BUYING FROM SUPERMARKETS

It can be a difficult transition from being able to buy everything in a shop to having to check every ingredient on foods, just in case – especially because many supermarkets do not specifically label things as suitable for vegans. One useful tip: if something is labelled vegetarian and has no allergens pointed out (eggs and dairy are both allergens, so would be in a bolder font), then it is pretty much guaranteed to be vegan. With sweet things, though, look out for honey. *Animal Free Shopper* is a great, pocket-sized guide, and can help with quick-reference queries.

# WHAT ABOUT WINE?

Many wines (and beers) are not suitable for vegans (or vegetarians) due to methods used in the fining process, which involves using fish, gelatine, egg white or milk proteins to remove yeast, proteins and other particles in the wine. There are vegan alternatives, however, and more companies are starting to label wines which are suitable for vegans. Generally, organic, natural wines are safe. The website: www.barnivore.com is a great resource for finding vegan-friendly wine and beer, as is the book *Animal Free Shopper*.

# VEGANISM IS NOT A 'SACRIFICE'. IT IS A JOY.

## GARY L. FRANCIONE

# Conclusion

I hope this little book has given you some insight into what it means to be vegan, as well as helpful hints, tips and recipes to make the transition an easier one. Remember: even a small change can be a powerful thing, so here's wishing you a happy, healthy move to a vegan lifestyle.

If you're interested in finding out more about our books, find us on Facebook at **SUMMERSDALE PUBLISHERS** and follow us on Twitter at **@SUMMERSDALE**.

**WWW.SUMMERSDALE.COM**